I Sink My Teeth Into Clover

I Sink My Teeth Into Clover

Mary Kibbe

Ink and Feet
Paris

First Published 2017

10 9 8 7 6 5 4 3 2 1

© Mary Kibbe 2017

Mary Kibbe has asserted her right
under the Copyright Act of 1976
to be identified as the author of this work.

First published in the United States in 2017
by Ink and Feet Press.
1603 N. Capitol Ave. #310A244, Cheyenne WY

For information on how to reproduce sections
of this book, write to publishing@marykibbe.com.

ISBN 0-9982804-3-7
ISBN-13 978-0-9982804-3-1

For the liminal spaces.

Contents

What if we let our shapes say everything?

The Languages I Don't Yet Speak: An Introduction	3
In the Cabinet of Fragile Things	5
At the Fruit Stand	7
This Part of You Lives Elsewhere	9
What Remains	11
Moon	13

Grief finds a way in and out.

Flexible	17
After the Funeral	19
Freezing Point	21
Past Curfew	23
Last Week's Puddle	25
He Never Said How	27

What isn't there to love about gravity?

9 Notes on Desire	31
The Irises Are in Bloom	33
Loneliness	35
Preparations	37
Upon Being Given a Dozen Roses That Had No Smell	39
Things Only the Full Moon and I Will Remember	41
Science	43
Notes & Acknowledgements	47

What if we let our shapes say everything?

The Languages I Don't Yet Speak: An Introduction

Between lightning and thunder is a story. The storm
that rumbles in the distance is caught in my lungs.
How can I tell you that it is getting closer?

This room, when you are in it, devours
all of my air. *Meet me*, I want to say,
but the letter *e* is stuck in my throat.

What if we let our shapes say everything?

I found the sliver of space between you and I
at the center of a labyrinth. If I hadn't tried
so hard to name it, would the space still move?

In the Cabinet of Fragile Things

You have rattled close to the edge.
The cleaning lady is here to dust.
She rubs a spot from your spine of glass,
runs you over with a feather,
sets you back to center.
She mutters and clucks, moves
to turn the blinds until light cracks
the room open. You'd like to stay where
everyone thinks you belong, but you can't.

At the Fruit Stand

You've forgotten his cheekbone, the angle
of his jaw, his blonde or brown hair

until the roadside fruit stand reminds you
of that first kiss at fifteen.

The juices linger
sloppy on your chin.

The sun dips into the hills.

Notice your pulse.

Remember—
not him

Remember you.
Still here.

This Part of You Lives Elsewhere

Clothes hung from a pine bough, she holds
her hair in the river until the sand beneath
her feet gives way. Voice lost to the girders
and bolt heads, under the fast-cycling
tires on the bridge overhead. No one
hears the revelry revealed to a sunless
sky, feels the salt dissolve on a hungry
tongue. Morning comes and she climbs
the brambled hillside, wanders until she finds
the wide skirt of a willow, long sleeves
dusting the road.

What Remains

Deeper than flesh, silt at the river's
bottom. Blood elements no longer mine.

I ask my tongue to do the washing.
Metal and mineral at the back of my throat.

Rain streams down the window's
other side. I press my face against

cold glass. The human body—
sixty-five percent water.

Moon

The moon holds the arches of my feet,
tosses me back into the water the way
my father did when I was small.

Grief finds a way in and out.

Flexible

More fiddlehead.
Soft coil, ruffled
green leaves, perched
atop an elegant stem
in a roadside ravine.

More snake.
Sundrenched
and curled to bake
on a flat desert
rock.

More slinky.
Agile as it plops
stair to stair.

Still, I am
the muddied
garden hose
hanging limp
against the house.

There are days
I am the spring
that slammed our
screen door closed
in summer.

Days I still want
to fly through
that door, without
caring if my shoes

are tied or not.

Days I miss
how often I was
wounded, skin torn
from knees, gravel dug
into my palms.

Up and running again,
too fast to think.

After the Funeral

The lone building has gone grey. The swollen ridges
of each grain of wood press deep into my fingertips.

The glass is gone, both windows open wide and unblinking
over a field of overgrown grass. The roof dips to one side

the way my father's torso did when I watched him walk away
with weight in his boots. Grief finds a way in and out.

Freezing Point

My insides and outsides
move at separate speeds.

This is the space I come back
to, when we are still

in motion. But there is no
traction on ice.

The impact is the same
as the day you stopped

holding my hand. The seatbelt
caught, the physical

weight of me yanked back.
The thermometer reads

thirty-two degrees.
Cold enough.

Past Curfew

Father was the cold metal handle
        the garage door slamming the last six inches
Mother was a furious spinner
        raw silk and entanglement pulled from the womb
He was the hatchet
She the one to wrap me at the chopping block.

Last Week's Puddle

An indented oval of clay earth dries
under a June sun. Last week, ankle deep
and lush with murky rainwater. I rolled
my pant legs and stepped in. Relished
the suction of my feet, the mud crawling
between my toes.

Today, all of the movement is in
the separation. Map of pieces,
edges curling back like our never
quite closed kitchen curtains.
At the right angle,

in the right light, one can imagine
connection. In an effort to not
disappear, I trace each fragment,
find a piece to lift and carry home.
Evidence to remind me
I've been here.

He Never Said How

Given the chance she would have saved every one,
laid them down in boxes, covered them in blankets
and only said *goodnight*. But you can't do that
with the dead. She's found a space for each of them.

The piles of broken bones collect against her ribs.
They glow like the ghosts they are against a red
pulse. She's tried to take them out:
plunged her hands in and pulled.

She called in a specialist to assist
with the removal but he shook his head.
He said *grieve*, he said *mourn*.

What isn't there to love about gravity?

9 Notes on Desire

It's more fingernail than fingertip as the hairdresser works conditioner against my scalp, and I have no choice but to remember.

In the spring, we were cartographers.

Words ran between us, thick and sticky as blood.

The air around us crackled.

The territory at the end of our nerves so much larger than the area where winter would take us.

It is not possible for the body to return to a blank slate state.

I sink my teeth into clover.

In the morning, I say yes to coffee and The New York Times.

As if there is anything to read but someone else's map.

The Irises Are in Bloom

The air is silk against my collarbones.
A tractor's engine runs all day long,
the steering wheel an itch beneath
my palms. There is no stopping
the days from getting longer.

I lay down on my grandmother's grave,
listen to the cut grass whisper, pretend
her breath against my cheek. The mailman
hasn't delivered a letter in three weeks.
I ask if perhaps she's forgotten to write.

I took scissors to the legs of my jeans
last night, loose threads tickle my thighs.
I ask if she ever feels desperate to press
her skin to someone else's, if she ever
loses track of her body like I do.

Loneliness

On the inside ankle
bone, an imprint
of lips, a shudder left
behind by the soft-
bristled brush of
beard against
skin, tightening
calves and an
ache at the back
of my knees.

Preparations

Lately, she's found
sleep best in the garden.
No fear of waking alone
when the dirt is so alive.

Parched by the empty house
that has never known how
to hold her, her body rests
in a bed of minerals.

Breath of a remembered
lover's lips swirls in cold,
October air. Silver-streaked
hair fans the ground, sweat

stains her deep-pocket
underarms. She slips into
dreams of earthworms,
a thousand fertilizer castings.

Upon Being Given a Dozen Roses That Had No Smell

Slice a piece of three-tiered cake
from the unlit display cooler.
Set the vase off center near the old register.

Here, on the row of dusty chairs,
I lie down with metal in my skin,
the scratch of wool, of running barelegged
against a sharp edged field of grass.

Make me a sculpture. Limbs
that twist and writhe, a bucket
of silver poured over me.

Things Only the Full Moon and I Will Remember

She was the kind of girl to stand in a doorway,
press the backs of her hands to the jambs on either side
and count to ten.

To open her eyes, spin a thread to mine across the room,
as her arms floated from her sides, the air parting her lips
on the way in.

To layer her body over mine and roll us across the hardwoods
to a rhythm I could only feel in the pressure of her limbs.

To sleep with a cupped hand over her heart,
afraid it would escape in the night.

Science

My skin doesn't hold
me, I say to the person who
always takes my calls.

I've worn the same
sweater for seven days straight.
I'm not ready to take it off.

He asks if I'd like to watch
the science channel. He's roasted
two quail. He'll make us a salad.

What isn't there to love about gravity?
My feet finding his floor, the bones of my thighs
saying yes to their hip sockets.

Notes & Acknowledgements

A lion's share of gratitude to Steven for innumerable layers of support, encouragement, and insight.

Pat, Darlene, Phyllis, Heidi—you continue to inspire me.

Some of these poems were first presented publicly at Slow Art PDX. I remain in awe of each of the artists who showed up each month to engage with the art and with each other. Steven, Robyn, Russ, Matt, Rayna, Jim. Thank you.

"Loneliness" originally appeared in *VoiceCatcher 6*. "The Languages I Don't Yet Speak: An Introduction" and "Freezing Point" enjoyed first publication in the Winter 2016 edition of Elohi Gadugi Journal. Deep appreciation and thanks goes out to the editors of those publications.

I was fortunate, in 2013, to receive the Baumeister Fellowship in Creative Writing from Fairleigh Dickinson University. The poems in this book represent a portion of the work that I created during my time in the MFA program there.

This book is typeset in Adobe Caslon Pro by Carol Twombly.

The cover design is by Ink and Feet Press.

The author photo was taken by Clara Fisher Johnson.

In both her professional life and her creative endeavors, Mary Kibbe is interested in the links between somatic experience, language, and healing. This is her first book of poems.

www.ingramcontent.com/pod-product-compliance
Lightning Source LLC
Chambersburg PA
CBHW070759020526
44118CB00036B/2134